Josie Granger

Finn and the Hidden Forest

Littlest Light Studio

lighting the way for dreamers, big and small.

Let me tell you a story. One about greed and destruction, but with a piece of hope. Hundreds of years ago, there was a magical forest. It was home to many kinds of beautiful trees and flowers.

However, once humans discovered the wood from the trees had magical abilities, they began chopping them down and destroying the forest out of their own greed. They left the forest with nothing but trampled flowers and tree stumps.

What the humans didn't realise, though, was that some magic remained in the tree stumps, which, as a last effort to save the once beautiful area, created woodland creatures to protect and regrow the forest. As they all began to wake up, the protector cast a spell to hide the forest from the humans.

As Finn came to the end of the story, he was shocked. "That can't be the end! What happened to the forest?" He thought as he flipped through the rest of the blank pages, looking for an answer.

As Finn drifted off to sleep, he began to dream.

He dreamt that he was walking through the pages of the book, exploring the illustrations, and trying to find the hidden forest to see it for himself.

He woke up with a burst of energy! He wanted to go outside and sketch what he could find. (Finn often did this when he felt inspired.) He packed his bag with everything he'd need.

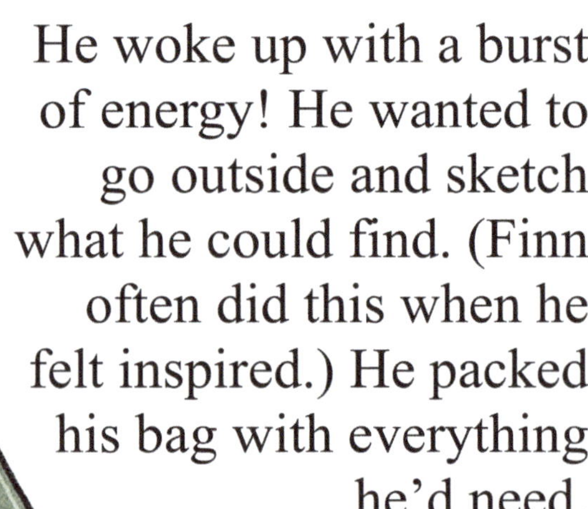

As the back door swung open, he looked ahead at the rolling green hills and thought, "I wonder what I'll find on my adventure."

Once Finn had set off, he found a sweet hedgehog and decided to sketch it in his book. After a little while, the hedgehog began to walk off, so he followed it to see where it was going.

Finn couldn't believe his eyes! After following the hedgehog for quite a while, it did something extremely odd; it seemed to walk through some kind of camouflaged barrier.

With great excitement, Finn followed the hedgehog and stepped through the magical barrier, and as he came through, he gazed across the beautiful forest. "It's the magic forest, from my book! I can't believe I've found it!" He shouted.

The woodland creatures were terrified! They froze up against the trees to try and hide. "How did a human boy get in?" said the magnolia tree. "What do we do?" said the silver birch tree as the protector of the forest stepped forward with his staff and said, "Who are you, and how did you enter our forest?"

"I am so sorry. I never meant to scare anyone; I followed that hedgehog who led me here," replied Finn timidly as he reached into his bag to hand him a gift.

"What are these?" asked the protector as he held the gift in his hand. "They are strawberries. You can eat them; they are fruit." Finn replied.

They started to walk together into the forest as the others came out of hiding. Along the way they spoke and got to know each other, the protector told Finn his name, Owen. Then they came across a beehive dripping with the most delicious-looking golden honey.

Finn asked the bees if they could spare some honey to eat, and they nodded and flew out of the way as Finn jumped up, using one of the bouncing flowers to collect it in his jar.

He jumped so high that he felt like he was flying!

Finn and Owen then joined the others for their picnic as Owen explained to them that they didn't need to fear Finn. They trusted Owen and proceeded to eat together. They all ate olives, petal soup, and Finn's strawberries dipped in the honey! It was delicious, and Finn loved getting to know them all as they introduced themselves properly.

"What does your forest look like?" Asked Bella. "My home isn't a forest; it's a house." Replied Finn as he began drawing his house to show them what he meant.

"He can draw things!" Shouted Samuel. Owen leapt up and, with great excitement, pulled out a pencil. "I already have a pencil though." Finn said with confusion. "Yes, but this pencil was carved out of the wood from one of our magical trees." Owen said as he handed it to Finn.

"What can it do?" Asked Finn. "Draw something with it in your book, and you'll see." Said Ollie. So, Finn drew some butterflies, and then Owen came over and blew on the page, and to Finn's amazement, his butterflies had blown off the page and had come to life!

Finn already had an idea of what to do with the pencil; he said to the others with joy, "I can make you all your very own houses!"

The others loved this idea, and as they walked to a clearing in the forest together, they discussed what a house is and what they'd all like.

Finn started to sketch the houses, designing each one
specifically and adding fun little details. These were some of
Finn's best drawings! He felt so proud of himself.

He blew onto the pages, and they all
stood back and watched as one-by-one
the houses became real with beautiful
twinkling lights and different shapes
of doors and windows.

As they all rushed to their new homes to explore, Owen turned to Finn and said, "I think you should draw yourself a home too; you are one of us now, and you have proven your heart is kind and pure, unlike the humans that came before you." "Thank you," replied Finn with a big smile.

He began to think about what kind of home he'd like to make for himself. He knew he'd like a desk inside where he could sit and draw and a big bookcase full of all his favourite stories, but he wasn't sure about much else yet.

Maggie said, "Your house should be made of flowers." and Orla said, "No, your house should have a big leaf on top to give you shade on hot, sunny days." Finn laughed as he began to draw the house that he decided he wanted.

The others looked at his drawing and watched as Finn blew on the page to add his very own home. Finally, the area felt complete.

They all played together and enjoyed their
new homes until the sun began to set and
the mushrooms and flowers began to glow
to light up the forest.

Finn knew he'd have to leave soon, so he wanted to end the day with something special. He decided to show his friends his favourite treat, so he sketched ingredients to make s'mores and lit a campfire using dry moss and leaves.

The s'mores were very tasty; they all sat around the campfire eating them while Finn discussed an idea he had to help protect the forest. "I could draw a wall to go behind the camouflaged barrier so that the forest isn't open as well as not being seen." "That is a brilliant idea, but how would you return?" Asked Owen. "I can make a door, and I'll keep the key." Replied Finn.

He headed for the opening as he drew the wall, which then surrounded the entire forest. It was made of strong, twisting branches and was very tall, so now people couldn't just walk through like Finn had.

He gave the pencil back to Owen. "I think you should keep this here; then I'll use it when I come to visit," said Finn. "I think you are very wise to not leave the forest with this; I'll keep it safe for you," replied Owen. "We are all going to miss you," said Ollie. Finn promised he'd return as he said goodbye to them all and began walking back.

Once Finn was home, he hung the key up on his pin board and then got cosy in his bed. As he began to fall asleep, he was happy thinking of all the fun he'd had with his new friends and looked forward to returning to the forest again soon.
THE END

Littlest Light Studio

lighting the way for dreamers, big and small.